Bicycle *Encyclopaedia*

C O N T E N T S

SWANMORE COUNTY
MIDDLE SCHOOL

Getting the most from this Encyclopaedia

This encyclopaedia contains information about the history, science, technology and sport of cycling. Different features of the encyclopaedia will help you look things up easily or to have fun just browsing through the entries.

All entries are in alphabetical order and there are several ways to find information on a topic.

Page headings
The page heading gives the first three letters of the first and last entries on that page.

The alphabetical index
This can be found at the back of the encyclopaedia. It lists the page numbers on which references to each entry are made.

The labelled bicycle
This can be found on **pages 30 and 31**. Next to each label are the page numbers you should turn to for more information on the topic.

Uni–Vel

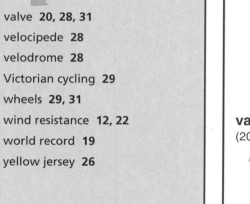

valve **20, 28, 31**

velocipede **28**

velodrome **28**

Victorian cycling **29**

wheels **29, 31**

wind resistance **12, 22**

world record **19**

yellow jersey **26**

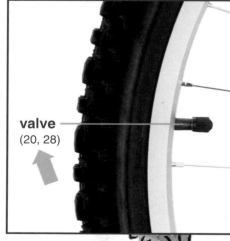

valve ———
(20, 28)

When you turn to an entry you will find some text which tells you the important facts. Most entries in the encyclopaedia also have a photograph. At the end of the text are cross-references. The cross-references show you that there is more information about the topic in other entries and you should look at them too.

Each entry has a symbol next to it. The symbols are used in the encyclopaedia to show when entries contain certain types of information:

 bicycle history

 bicycle safety

 bicycle maintenance and parts

 racing and competitions

general bicycle information

types of bicycle

A

B

 Axle

An axle is the rod or bar through the middle of the wheel. A bicycle's wheels are fastened to the frame by nuts on the ends of the axles.

➤ **see labelled bicycle, pages 30-31**

 Ball bearing

Steel ball bearings are used inside the moving parts of a bicycle to make them turn smoothly. The ball bearings are packed with grease to reduce friction.

 see also: bottom bracket; friction; headset; hub

⭐ **Bicycle**

The word 'bicycle' means 'two wheels'. The first bicycles were built in the 1820s. They did not have pedals and were called hobby horses. The modern bicycle or bike is the most efficient means of transport ever invented. Travelling by bicycle uses just a third of the energy of walking. It does not burn fuel so it does not cause pollution. The exercise is healthy and cycling is much cheaper than travelling by car. It is usually much quicker to travel by bicycle than by bus or taxi in busy towns and cities. There are now more than 800 million bicycles throughout the world, more than double the number of cars.

 see also: hobby horse

BMX bike

BMX stands for 'bicycle motor cross'. BMX bikes are specially designed for rough, dirt-track riding. BMX racing started in the United States in the 1970s. BMX stunting is a popular sport, too. BMX bikes have chunky wheels and extra strong frames made from a shiny metal called 'cro-mo'.

> **see also: mountain bike; off road bikes**

Stunting on a BMX bike

Boardman, Chris

Chris Boardman is one of Britain's top racing cyclists. In 1992 he won an Olympic gold medal. He rode a Lotus superbike specially designed for high-speed track racing. Now he is a professional cyclist and rides in the Tour de France.

> **see also: racing bike; frame; Tour de France; Obree, Graham**

6

Boneshaker

Boneshaker was the nickname given to the first pedal-powered bicycle. These early machines had solid rubber tyres on metal wheels. They gave a very rough ride over cobbled streets and made the rider's bones shake.

Bottom bracket

The bottom bracket is the joint at the bottom of the bicycle frame where the pedals and cranks are fixed. Ball bearings inside the bracket make the cranks turn smoothly.

 see also: ball bearing; crank; frame; pedals

➤ **see labelled bicycle, pages 30-31**

Brakes

Effective brakes are vital for bicycle safety. The brakes are operated by squeezing brake levers on the handle bars. The brake cable pulls on lever arms which press rubber brake blocks on to the wheel rim. Friction slows the wheel down. Bicycle brakes do not work well in the rain because water reduces the friction. Extra care should be taken when braking in wet conditions. Brakes should be checked and adjusted regularly. Worn brake blocks must be replaced.

 see also: cables; friction; maintenance; safety

➤ **see labelled bicycle, pages 30-31**

Burton, Beryl

Beryl Burton has won more championships than any other British cyclist. She was British ladies time trial champion 25 times between 1959 and 1983.

 See also: time trial

Beryl Burton

C

Cables

Cables connect the brake and gear levers to the brakes and gears on the wheels. The outside of the cable is a plastic and metal tube. A steel wire moves inside the tube when the levers are pulled.

 see also: brakes; gears

➤ **see labelled bicycle, pages 30-31**

Chain

The chain carries the force from the cyclist's legs pushing on the pedals, to the back wheel. The links of the chain are connected by rollers to help reduce friction. The links fit neatly over the teeth on the chain wheel and sprockets.

 see also: chain wheel; friction; sprocket

➤ **see labelled bicycle, pages 30-31**

Chain wheel

The large toothed cog turned by the pedals.

 see also: chain; pedals

➤ **see labelled bicycle, pages 30-31**

⚡ Clothing

Clothing must keep a cyclist warm and dry without making him or her overheat. Bright colours are easily seen by motorists and help with safety. Cycling shirts and shorts are made from stretch fabrics such as Lycra® so that the rider can move easily. Cycling shorts have no seams where they might rub on the saddle. In cold, wet weather a wind-proof jacket is essential to keep the cyclist warm.

see also: helmet; safety

 ## Cog

A cog is a toothed wheel that can be turned by a chain. Also called a sprocket.

see also: chain; chain wheel; gears; sprocket

 ## Crank

The crank is the bar that connects the pedal to the chain wheel.

see also: chain; pedals

➤ **see labelled bicycle, pages 30-31**

helmet

reflective strips

wind-proof jacket

cycling shorts

⚡ Cycle ways

Cycle ways are special paths or tracks reserved for cyclists. Cycling is an important means of transport but it can be dangerous to mix bicycles, cars and lorries on the same road. Some town and city councils have built cycle ways to encourage cycling and cut down traffic jams. There are plans for long distance cycle ways through the countryside. There is already a cycle track between Bristol and Bath which is used for a million journeys each year.

⚡ Cycling proficiency

The cycling proficiency test checks children's basic cycling and road user skills. Children are trained to get on and off a bicycle safely, to give the correct signals and to obey the rules of the road. They learn how to check that their brakes are working properly and when they need lights. They must answer questions about road signs and the highway code. When they pass they receive a badge and a certificate.

 see also: safety

Cyclo-cross

Cyclo-cross is an exciting bicycle sport. The cyclists race across muddy tracks, through woods and over streams. Often it is quicker to put your bike on your shoulder and run than to stay on it and keep pedalling!

 see also: mountain bike

D

Dunlop, John Boyd

John Boyd Dunlop developed the pneumatic (air-filled) tyre in 1888. One day he was watching his son playing on a tricycle fitted with solid rubber tyres. The tricycle looked very uncomfortable as it bumped over the cobbled streets. Dunlop had the idea of making tyres from pieces of tubing pumped full of air. The air-filled pneumatic tyres acted like springy cushions over the bumps. They made the tricycle much more comfortable. Dunlop started a factory to make pneumatic tyres. Today the Dunlop company makes millions of tyres each year for all kinds of wheeled vehicles including bicycles.

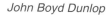 see also: tyres; wheels

John Boyd Dunlop

F

Forks

The front forks of a bicycle hold the front wheel. They connect the wheel to the handle bars so that the rider can steer the bicycle. The forks are usually curved and sloped forwards. This makes the bike easier to balance and steer.

> **see also: frame**

➤ **see labelled bicycle, pages 30-31**

Frame

A bicycle frame must be stiff, light and strong. Standard bike frames are made from hollow metal tubes put together in the shape of a double triangle. New ultra-light materials such as carbon fibre are used for some frames. These frames can be as light as four kilograms. Chris Boardman rode a Lotus bike when he won the Olympic medal. This bike has a completely new frame design called a monocoque. It is made from carbon fibre. Its special shape cuts down wind resistance and makes the bike much faster.

The lotus superbike

A standard bicycle

⭐ Friction

Friction stops things from sliding smoothly over each other. It is both the cyclist's enemy and friend. Friction in the wheel hubs, chain and gears wastes energy. Ball bearings, grease and oil help to cut down the friction in these parts to make the movement smooth and efficient. Friction is needed between the tyres and the road to stop skids. It is also needed between the brake blocks and the wheels to slow the bicycle down.

 # Future bicycles

In the future more lightweight materials will be used to make bicycles. Body shells may be added to cut down wind resistance. A recumbent bicycle with its body shell can travel at more than 95 kilometres an hour. Electric bikes such as the Sinclair Zike may become popular too. Experimental solar powered bicycles work well in Australia. They will probably not be successful in Britain where the sun does not shine as much.

'Stinger' bike

▶ **see also: recumbent bicycle**

A recumbent bicycle with body shell

G

 # Gears

The gears on a bicycle change the speed at which the back wheel turns when the pedals are pushed. Racing bikes and mountain bikes have derailleur gears. Moving the gear lever shifts the chain between cogs with different numbers of teeth. A low gear is selected to go uphill. High gears are used for speeding along on a flat road.

 see also: chain; cogs

H

 # Head tube

The head tube is the part of the frame through which the tube on the end of the forks passes. Inside the head tube a set of ball bearings called the head set make the forks turn smoothly.

 see also: ball bearing; forks; frame

> **see labelled bicycle, pages 30-31**

 # Helmet

A helmet protects a rider's head in an accident. Road accidents involving cyclists are common, especially in towns. Without a helmet a fall from a bicycle can lead to serious head injuries. Cyclists should always wear a safety helmet. A good helmet is very light and has air holes to keep the rider cool.

 **see also: clothing; safety**

Johnson, the First Rider on the Pedestrian Hobbyhorse.

 # Hobby horse

Hobby horses were the first bicycles. They were invented in 1817 by a German baron called Karl von Drais. Hobby horses did not have pedals, the riders pushed them along with their feet.

 see also: velocipede

 # Hub

The hub is the centre of a wheel. It is packed inside with ball bearings and grease so that the wheel turns smoothly. The hub is usually connected to the wheel rim by spokes.

 see also: spokes; wheel
  ➤ **see labelled bicycle, pages 30-31**

 ## Inner tube

A rubber inner tube is used to line a tyre. The inner tube is completely air-tight. It stops air escaping from inside the tyre when it is pumped up.

 see also: tyre

 ## Lights

Bicycle lights must be used when riding at night. The front light is white and the back light is red. Lights can be powered by batteries or a dynamo. Battery powered lights are safer because they shine all the time. A dynamo is turned by the wheel so the lights go out when the bike stops at a junction.

 see also: safety

▲ Battery operated lights

◄ Dynamo operated light

 ## Locks

Lock it or lose it! Sadly, bicycle theft is very common. A good lock has a steel cable or chain that is difficult to cut. The chain should be passed through the bicycle wheels and around a post or cycle rack for extra security.

A modern photograph of the first bike with pedals.

 ## Macmillan, Kirkpatrick

Kirkpatrick Macmillan invented the first bicycle with pedals in 1840. In 1842 in the city of Glasgow he was involved in the first known bicycling accident. Macmillan rode into a crowd of people and knocked down a child.

I

L

M

 ## Maintenance

Regular maintenance keeps a bicycle safe and running smoothly. Brakes should be checked and worn brake blocks replaced. The chain should be cleaned and lubricated. Modern bicycle parts should not be oiled too much. The oil attracts dirt and grit which wears the parts out quickly.

 see also: safety

 ## Moulton, Alex

Alex Moulton invented the small-wheeled Moulton bike in 1962. Small wheels give a rough ride over bumpy ground but Moulton solved this problem by including springs and rubber suspension in his design. Moulton racing bicycles are now amongst the most advanced bicycles made.

Small-wheeled Moulton bicycles

 ## Mountain bike

Mountain bikes are now the most popular kind of bicycle. They were first made for racing and touring on rough mountain tracks in the USA. Now they are popular for all types of cycling both in town and country. They have small frames for comfort, tough wheels with thick tyres to ride over rough ground and up to 24 gears. Some of the gears are very low to climb steep hills.

 see also: BMX bike

⭐ Murphy, Dervla

Dervla Murphy from Ireland has made some fantastic journeys by bicycle. Her first expedition was in 1962 when she cycled all the way from Ireland to India. In 1992, at the age of 60, she cycled more than 4500 kilometres through Africa on a mountain bike.

 see also: mountain bike

Dervla Murphy

O

P

 # Obree, Graham

In July 1993, Graham Obree from Scotland set a new world record for a one hour time trial. He cycled 51596 metres in one hour on an indoor track. He beat the previous record, which had stood for nine years, by 445 metres. Obree used a bicycle he had made himself using parts from an old washing machine! Obree's new record was beaten just a few days later by Chris Boardman and has since been beaten several times by other riders.

Graham Obree on his special bicycle.

 # Off road bikes

Off road bikes such as BMX and mountain bikes are tough machines designed to ride on rough ground. They usually have chunky tyres to smooth out the bumps and provide grip on slippery tracks.

 see also: BMX bike; mountain bike

 # Pedals

Pedals are the platforms the cyclist's feet push to turn the wheels.

➤ **see labelled bicycle, pages 30-31**

 # Penny farthing

Penny farthing was the nick name for high-wheeled bikes built a hundred years ago. The proper name for a penny farthing was the 'ordinary' bicycle. The large front wheel made the ordinary fast without the need for gears. Racing them was popular but they were difficult to ride. Getting on an ordinary was hard and it was easy to tip over the handle bars coming downhill.

 see also: Starley, James

 # Police bicycle

A policeman patrolling on a bicycle was once a common sight. Then the police started using patrol cars and police bicycles became less common. Now they are coming back into use. These days a policeman is more likely to patrol on a high-tech mountain bike than an old fashioned bicycle. Policemen in the USA can chase criminals more quickly on a mountain bike than in a car through crowded city streets.

 see also: mountain bike

Pump

A pump is used to blow up bicycle tyres. The pump pushes air through the valve.

 see also: tyres; valve

Puncture

A puncture is a hole in a tyre which lets the air escape. Rubber tyres are easily punctured by an old nail or a sharp thorn. A puncture repair kit with stick on rubber patches is essential for a long journey by bike.

 see also: tyres

Pursuit racing

Pursuit racing takes place on a cycle track or velodrome. Two individuals or teams start on opposite sides of the track and try to catch their rivals as they speed around.

 see also: racing bike; velodrome

Pursuit racing on a velodrome

Racing bike

Racing bikes are very light and very fast. Thin wheels and tyres cut down friction with the ground but they can only be ridden on smooth surfaces or the wheels buckle. Racing bikes don't have mudguards or lights. This keeps them as light as possible. Road racing bikes have brakes and gears but track racing bikes don't have either. A track bike weighs less than nine kilograms.

Recumbent bicycle

The rider of a recumbent bicycle sits down with their legs facing forwards. Recumbent cycles look odd but they are actually faster than ordinary bicycles because there is less wind resistance. Some recumbent bicycles have a flag on the back which helps them to be seen in traffic.

 see also: future bicycles

Reflectors

Reflectors on a bike make it show up at night in the headlights of traffic. Reflective strips on the cyclist's clothing are also an excellent safety feature.

 see also: safety

➤ **see labelled bicycle, pages 30-31**

S

 # Saddle

The saddle is the bicycle's seat. Different shaped saddles suit different shaped people. Some saddles have springs for comfort. Racing saddles are very thin to reduce friction with the legs. Leather saddles can be quite hard. Some modern saddles are filled with gel to make them more comfortable.

➤ **see labelled bicycle, pages 30-31**

R

S

Safety

Bicycles are very fast so they can be dangerous unless they are ridden correctly. To be safe on their bicycles cyclists should always:

- wear a helmet

- wear brightly coloured clothes so that they can be seen easily

- use lights in the dark

- maintain their bicycle so that the brakes work and all the parts run smoothly

- learn the highway code and obey the rules of the road.

 see also: brakes; clothing; helmet; cycling proficiency

Learning the highway code

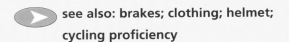 # Safety bicycle

The 'safety' bicycle was invented in 1884 by John Starley. It was the first bicycle with a geared chain drive like a modern bicycle. The gearing meant that it was fast without the need for a large wheel like the penny farthing. It was easier and safer to ride than a penny farthing and so became known as the 'safety'.

see also: penny farthing; Starley, James; Starley, John

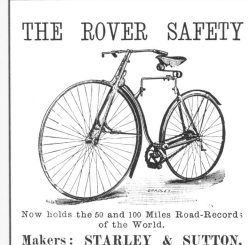

THE ROVER SAFETY

Now holds the 50 and 100 Miles Road-Records of the World.

Makers: **STARLEY & SUTTON,**
WEST ORCHARD, COVENTRY.
Send for Lists.

Spokes

Wire spokes connect the wheel hub to the wheel rim. The spokes can be adjusted by tightening them one at a time to make sure that the wheel is perfectly round.

 see also: hub; wheel

➤ see labelled bicycle, pages 30-31

 # Sprocket

Sprockets are the toothed wheels or cogs turned by the chain.

 see also: chain wheel; cog; gears

➤ see labelled bicycle, pages 30-31

 # Starley, James

Invented the ordinary bicycle, or 'Penny farthing', in 1870.

 see also: penny farthing

 # Starley, John

Invented the safety bicycle in 1884. James Starley's nephew.

 see also: safety bicycle

James Starley

T

S

T

 **Tandem**

A tandem is a bicycle made for two. The front rider is the captain and the rear rider is the stoker. Tandems are faster than solo bikes.

 Time trial

A time trial is a race against the clock. Riders are timed to see how long it takes to cover a fixed distance or to see how far they can ride in a set time.

> **see also: Burton, Beryl; Obree, Graham; racing bike**

 Toe clips

Toe clips keep the ball of the foot on the pedal. This is the best part of the foot to use to get a powerful push. Racing cyclists wear special shoes that actually clip on to the pedals.

> **see also: pedals**

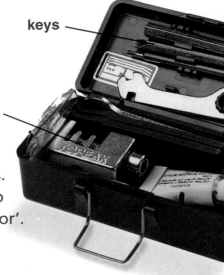

keys

link extractor

 ## Tools

The only tools needed to do most jobs on a modern bicycle are a few spanners and keys. A special tool is required to break a chain to replace worn links. It is called a 'link extractor'.

 ## Tour de France

The Tour de France is the most famous cycling race in the world. It lasts for three weeks. On most days of the Tour the riders race for more than 160 kilometres. During the race the leader wears the yellow jersey. The king of the mountains (the fastest rider up the steep mountain sections of the tour) wears a polka dot jersey. The green jersey is worn by the rider with the most points from the special sprint stages. The race always finishes under the Arc de Triomphe in Paris. The winner of the Tour can claim to be best cyclist in the world.

 see also: **racing bike**

Touring

Bicycle touring is one of the very best ways to explore the countryside. A tour can last a day with a picnic packed in a ruck sack. On a touring holiday, cyclists take camping gear and spare clothes packed in panniers on their bikes.

Tricycle

A tricycle is a cycle with three wheels. Tricycles are more stable and easier to ride than bicycles but they are slower and difficult to steer. Tricycles are good for carrying heavy loads. In the past they have been used to sell ice-cream and deliver groceries.

Tyres

Modern bicycle tyres are pneumatic (inflated with air). The spring of the tyre helps to cushion bumps. The rubber treads grip the ground. Thick, deep-treaded tyres are used for rough ground. Thin tyres are much faster over smooth ground.

▷ see also: **Dunlop, John Boyd; hub; spokes; wheel**

➤ **see labelled bicycle, pages 30-31**

 Unicycle

A unicycle is a cycle with one wheel. Unicycles are difficult to balance on and are mainly used by acrobats and clowns to perform tricks.

 Valve

The valve on a bicycle inner tube lets in air from the pump and then stops it escaping. A spring holds the valve closed keeping the air inside the tyre.

 see also: inner tube; pump; tyres
 see labelled bicycle, pages 30-31

 Velocipede

Velocipede was the French name for the first bicycles without pedals, called hobby horses in England. Velocipede means 'fast feet'. Later velocipedes were fitted with pedals.

 see also: hobby horse

 Velodrome

A velodrome is a special track for cycle racing. The riders race at high speed. The curves on the track are sloped or banked to stop the bicycles from skidding as they speed around the bends.

 see also: pursuit racing; racing bike; time trial

U

V

W

Victorian cycling

Cycling first became a popular hobby in the Victorian times, with the invention of the ordinary and safety bicycles. Both ladies and gentlemen bicycled. Many ladies wore knickerbockers or bloomers to cycle instead of their long skirts. This was considered very daring.

➤ see also: penny farthing; safety bicycle

Fashionable Victorian cyclists

Wheels

Bicycle wheels must be strong but light. Most bicycle wheels are made with wire spokes which connect the hub to the rim. The rim is the metal hoop to which the tyre is fixed. Some modern wheels are solid or have three broad spokes. These cut through the air more easily than wire spokes.

➤ see also: hub; spoke; tyre
➤ see labelled bicycle, pages 30-31

Labelled bicycle

saddle (22)

spokes
(15, 24)

reflector
(22)

sprockets (cogs)
(8, 9, 14, 24)

pedal
(5, 7, 8, 9, 15,
17, 19, 25, 28)

chain
wheel
(8, 9)

tyre
(13, 16, 19, 20, 21, 27)

chain
(8, 13, 14,
17, 24, 26)

crank
(7, 9)

bottom
bracket
(7)

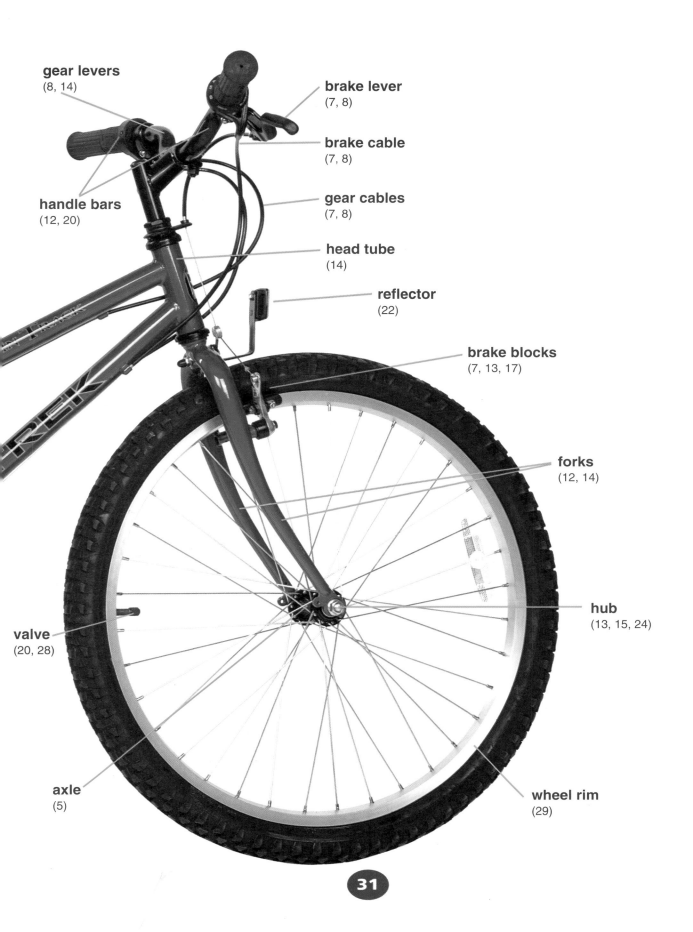

gear levers
(8, 14)

brake lever
(7, 8)

brake cable
(7, 8)

gear cables
(7, 8)

head tube
(14)

handle bars
(12, 20)

reflector
(22)

brake blocks
(7, 13, 17)

forks
(12, 14)

hub
(13, 15, 24)

valve
(20, 28)

axle
(5)

wheel rim
(29)

Index